Popcorn Elder

Popcorn Elder

Curtis Peeteetuce

Popcorn Elder
first published 2018 by Scirocco Drama
An imprint of J. Gordon Shillingford Publishing Inc.

Scirocco Drama Editor: Glenda MacFarlane

Cover design by Terry Gallagher/Doowah Design
Cover photo by m.pet productions
from the series "Indian in the coffee shop"
model: Rylan Smallchild

Author photo by Aloys Neil Mark Fleischmann (Festivale Media)
Production photos by Britainy Zapshalla

Printed and bound in Canada on 100% post-consumer recycled paper.
We acknowledge the financial support of the Manitoba Arts Council and
The Canada Council for the Arts for our publishing program.

Production inquiries should be addressed to:
curtispeeteetuce@gmail.com

Library and Archives Canada Cataloguing in Publication

Peeteetuce, Curtis, author
Popcorn elder / Curtis Peeteetuce. -- First edition.

A play.
ISBN 978-1-927922-39-2 (softcover)

I. Title.

PS8631.E399P67 2018 C812'.6 C2018-900237-9

J. Gordon Shillingford Publishing
P.O. Box 86, RPO Corydon Avenue, Winnipeg, MB Canada R3M 3S3

Dedicated to the many fathers and sons
whose story is too often untold;
to our women so strong and courageous;
and to those that still need healing.

In loving memory

Anpetu Wi Wanmdi Hoksina
(Bradley Adam Buffalo)
May 1985 – October 2015

Rest In Peace
Love, your family

Curtis Peeteetuce

Curtis is from the Beardy's and Okemasis Cree Nation. Since 2001, he has had the honour of working with many talented artists in theatre, radio drama, music and film. Selected highlights include Theatre Prospero / Akpik Theatre (*Pawâkan Macbeth*), Shakespeare on the Saskatchewan (*Richard III, Twelfth Night*), Globe Theatre (*Salt Baby*), Persephone Theatre (*A History of Breathing*) and GTNT (*Where the Blood Mixes, Thunderstick*).

Curtis is the recipient of the Saskatoon and Area Theatre Award for Outstanding Male Performance and the Henry Woolf Award for Achievement. He is also the playwright of the Rez Christmas story series, including *Nicimos: The Final Rez Christmas Story* (Scirocco, 2015.)

Curtis dedicates all his efforts and accomplishments to his son Mahihkan. *Nanaskimonawaw.*

Acknowledgements

Thank you to:
Gordon Tootoosis Nikaniwin Theatre
Dancing Sky Theatre
Playwrights Theatre Centre
Saskatchewan Playwrights Centre

My love and heart to the many artists and friends who have shared their gifts in the development of *Popcorn Elder* at the 2014 Spring Festival of New Plays: Carol Greyeyes, Kenneth T. Williams, Kent Allen, Dawn Bird, Mark Dieter.

Also love to the cast of the workshop reading at the Playwrights Theatre Centre 2014 Residency: Kathleen Flaherty (dramaturge), Maureen Labonte (guest dramaturge), Larry Grant (language consultant), Sam Bob, Evan Frayne, Curtis Ahenakew, Andrea Menard, Quelemia Sparrow.

Playwright's Notes

In 2009, in Arizona, the American self-improvement salesman James Arthur Ray charged people up to $10,000 to take part in his idea of a sweat lodge. Three died, and eighteen were hospitalized. Ray was sentenced to two years in prison.

As soon as I heard that, I was furious. I was angry; I was hurt.

I realized that I could either post my thoughts on Facebook for a brief reaction, or I could leverage my feelings with the power of art. Instead of posting to social media, I channelled my feelings through my gifts of writing and theatre, where the story could have a bigger life and a longer-lasting impact.

This is the inspiration behind *Popcorn Elder.*

Production History

Popcorn Elder by Curtis Peeteetuce

A co-production between
Gordon Tootoosis Nikaniwin Theatre
and Dancing Sky Theatre

Premiered April 29 to May 16, 2016 at Dancing Sky Theatre, Meacham, Saskatchewan, with a subsequent run from May 19 to 29, 2016 at Gordon Tootoosis Nikaniwin Theatre, Saskatoon, Saskatchewan.

Cast

Wally Marten, Ben .... Sam Bob

Darren Kihew .... Cory Standing

Arthur Bear .... Bruce Sinclair

Cindy, Alice, Cheyenne, Kelly...... Krystle Pederson

Madge, Serena, Heather.......................... Wanita Bird

Director: Angus Ferguson

Stage Management:
Kenilee Kehler, Angela Christie

Set Design: Angus Ferguson

Costume Design: Jeff Chief

Lighting Design: Kenilee Kehler

Sound Design: Anthony Orr

Left to right: Krystle Pederson, Bruce Sinclair and Wanita Bird.

Left to right: Cory Standing and Sam Bob.

Left to right: Cory Standing and Sam Bob.

Left to right: Cory Standing, Sam Bob,
Krystle Pederson, Bruce Sinclair and Wanita Bird.

Cast

DARREN Kihew .... Cree male, 30s
WALLY Marten .... Cree male, late 50s, DARREN's dad
ARTHUR Bear .... Male, late 50s
CINDY Isbister.. Métis female, 30
MADGE Tipiskaw .... Cree female, late 50s
ALICE..Female, 30s
BEN .... Male, 50s, Alice's father
CHEYENNE Bear .... Cree female, 5,
ARTHUR's granddaughter
SERENA Iskotew ....Cree female, 5, Cheyenne's friend
HEATHER.. Cree female, 30s, cop
KELLY .... White female, 30s, cop

Setting

Present day. Stone Pipe First Nation, Saskatchewan.

Locations include: WALLY's house, high school, an alley, a clearing, and a cafe.

ACT I

Scene 1

WALLY Marten's house on Stone Pipe First Nation. DARREN grabs a beer from the fridge. The phone rings.

DARREN: Hello?

Who's this?

Oh, hi…

What do you mean, "it's about damn time"? Nice to hear from you, too, Cindy.

Where was I? Really? Like what the –

Where do you think? I –

I just got out! Really?

On the reserve! Holy, woman.

DARREN pulls the phone away from his ear. There is incoherent loudness on the other end of the phone.

No, I didn't go to ceremony just to get out early. As if you have to say that. Well, your tone of voice, I –

All right! Okay! Yes, I said –

Give me a goddamn second to talk, okay?

I spent everything I had to get here. I –

No. Just listen –

DAMMIT!

CINDY again. Sound of incoherent yelling.

Let me talk to him.

Who? Michel! My son, who else?!

Oh yeah...school, right.

Well I've been gone –

I wasn't even drunk –

Here on Stone Pipe, they said –

My dad's! Where else?!

CINDY, again, incoherent but loud.

I have to live here because the reserve is the only place I can get a job. My cousin Brad set it up. I already have steel-toed boots. Starts Monday.

CINDY, again.

I HAVE A JOB; I'm not going back!

My temper? Mine? You're the one with –

I wasn't gonna say bipolar, holy, I –

Yeah, yeah... If I couldn't tolerate you at your worst, then I don't deserve you at your best.

Pause, then CINDY: "Well?"

Thing is, woman...

CINDY: "What?"

AfterallthesefuckingyearsIgottiredofwaitingto-seeyourbest!

DARREN hangs up the phone. He drinks.

Always brings out the worst in me.

Pfft. Ceremony...

He notices a small black pan. Four people enter, dressed in the colour of the current season: the men in shorts, the women in gowns. They all sit on the floor holding towels. An elder opens a suitcase. He emulates smudging while whispering in Cree. Everyone in the circle is quiet. ARTHUR breaks the ice.

ARTHUR: *Ahaw.* Sit down, boy. Right here.

DARREN: Where's my dad?

ARTHUR: CLOSE THE DOOR, *oskapew.* (helper.) Shh. Thank you all for coming. Welcome. My name is Arthur, but my Indian name is Sacred Wind Man and – hey. No. Not like that, like this. See? Start from the north, then work your way back around. Clockwise, then pass it on. Good. Good boy, this one. Smart. Should make a good husband and father someday. Make sure, ladies, your daughters snag him now. Heyyyyy. After this we'll eat ceremonial berries. (*ARTHUR gestures to the next person.)* You hold the pan this round. *(To another person.)* In round three, you'll hold it. Okay, it's time. Let's begin. *Ahaw.* Time to invite the spirits in. We will begin by praying. Praying to the Great Mystery. Inviting the spirits of all directions to watch over us during this holy sweat lodge. The sound of the drum is a stampede for healing, from the spirits of Grandmother and Grandfather Buffalo. We are thankful. *Ahaw.* Okay, pray. Pray, all of you…

The sound of a rattle accompanies prayer and song. DARREN stares at ARTHUR as everyone else bows and prays. In an instant it's quiet and everyone exits. ARTHUR looks back at DARREN before his exit. Everyone but DARREN exits. He puts the pan down, noticing his dad, WALLY Marten, staring.

WALLY: Want some help?

DARREN: Huh?

WALLY: Looks like you're tryna smudge.

DARREN: No. Just...looking – what the hell? Put some clothes on!

WALLY: Relax. Just got out of the shower. Good morning, by the way.

DARREN: Yeah…

WALLY: Ran out of gas this morning. Had to pull out the jerry can in the back and walk to Morley's. Damn dusty out there.

DARREN: Morley's is still open?

WALLY: Yeah. Only gas station on the rez. Good thing. Where'd the beer come from?

DARREN: Brad. A "getting out" gift.

WALLY: You're not supposed to drink.

DARREN: It's only three beer.

WALLY: Only takes one. I picked up the newspaper in town.

WALLY dries himself and puts on a shirt and socks. The phone rings.

DARREN: I suppose it's Cindy. Look on the call display. Does it say "Isbister"?

WALLY: Yeah.

DARREN answers the call and hangs up immediately.

Did you sleep good?

DARREN: Yeah. Ya know, Wally, the things we take for granted. Like mattresses. That pull-out is great.

WALLY: I can imagine.

DARREN: Man, does that woman ever hate me.

A knock on the door. Enter MADGE.

WALLY: *PIHTIKWE.* (Come inside.)

MADGE: *Aha, tanisi kahkiyaw?* (How are you all?)

WALLY: *Aha, Makitohn* (Big Mouth), Madge. *Tanisi kīya iskwew?* (How are you, lady?)

MADGE: *Moya nanitaw. Kiya maka,* Wally? (Not bad, and yourself?)

WALLY: *Peyakwan.* (Same.)

MADGE: *Eee wah hua,* is that Darren? You're finally home.

DARREN: Hi, Madge.

MADGE: *Kayas* (Long ago), Darren. Good to see you.

DARREN: Good to see you, too.

MADGE: You're still such a handsome man. *Tanisi kīya, napew?* (How are you, man?)

DARREN: Good. Thanks.

MADGE: When's the last time you saw Michel?

DARREN: Before I went in…

MADGE: I ran into Cindy at Superstore in the city. Then to Chuck E. Cheese for Michel's birthday. She didn't talk much. Is that where she lives now?

DARREN: Beats me.

MADGE: Well, I did remind her where I live and said she can stop in anytime. With your son.

DARREN: Cool. Thanks. If you find out when she'll let me see Michel, let me know. So how have you been?

MADGE: I've been so busy this summer. Mostly on the ceremony trail, visiting, listening, learning. It's good, but I can't handle all the travel. Wish I could be in one place.

WALLY: Taking on the world, eh, Madge?

MADGE: I'll always come back to visit. Oh, Wally, I haven't had time to start building the winter lodge. I was wondering if you could help me out with that. I think you're about ready now.

WALLY: Me?

DARREN: Him?

WALLY: Hey. Me? *Tapwe ci?* (It's true?)

MADGE: Mm-hm.

WALLY: Wow. Cool. Sure, we can help out.

DARREN: We? Hey, wait –

WALLY: What do you need?

MADGE: *Ah hei hei.* (Thank you.) Here's the tobacco and cloth.

DARREN: What's happening?

MADGE hands WALLY a pack of cigarettes. They shake hands.

WALLY: *Aha, tapwe.*

MADGE: Thank you, Wally. Good to see you doing better. There'll be lots to do. Rocks, wood, willow. But not today. I have to be at the school. There's a feast today. You should come.

WALLY: Uh, yeah.

DARREN: Hey, I didn't say I'd – wait, better?

MADGE: Oh, and also, did you get that blanket?

WALLY: Oh, yeah. It's in the other room. *Ceskwa.* (Wait.)

MADGE: *Miywasin.* (It's good.) I'm taking it for the giveaway.

WALLY exits.

So? Out of the slammer, eh?

DARREN: Uh, yeah, just got out – or I mean back, last night. Stuck here for the next year at least.

MADGE: And you and Cindy broke up while you were away.

DARREN: Yeah. Madge, I'm embarrassed to say I haven't seen my boy in a couple years. Even you know more than I do.

MADGE: I know. He's still young…there's still time. By now you must have a better handle on your emotions.

DARREN: I do, but not her. You don't know Cindy the way I do.

MADGE: I know it can be hard. Just keep Michel in mind.

DARREN: I will. Pfft, "Michel." Who names their boy that? "Michael," I told her. He's not French.

MADGE: Michif. I did tell her to take him to the doctor for regular check-ups. It's good to stay informed of these as well as traditional ways. Lots of kids sick this past year. *Wacistakac.* (An expression of surprise.)

DARREN: Yeah, in the pen, too. Man, I didn't want to be around anyone. No way. Just stayed in my cell all the time and read.

MADGE: Did you hear about that one woman?

DARREN: No. Which one?

MADGE: I didn't hear much. But a woman got taken in by a con artist. Just over a year ago, I think.

DARREN: What happened?

MADGE: Apparently she contacted a so-called medicine man to help her dad.

DARREN: Really?

MADGE: Uh huh. But just when she met her dad and moved up north to be with him, he gets sick. They go to the doctor, doctors don't know what to do.

DARREN: Geez.

MADGE: They sent her home. Her dad gets worse, so she somehow gets hold of this medicine man, who goes in, does a couple of prayers and chants, then leaves.

Transition. In the dark, guitar music plays. A chorus of voices sings a quiet song. ARTHUR enters and sits. A middle-aged man is sick with serious symptoms. His daughter sits beside him. They both have white masks on.

ARTHUR: My name is Arthur. But my Indian name is Sacred Wind Man.

Beat.

Originally I was supposed to be in the city tonight with an old friend, but I got your message. It was good of you to inbox me. Told me your father is sick and that it's an emergency. So I'm here. But I'll have to leave right after this.

As ARTHUR whispers a prayer, the woman stands.

ALICE: I don't know if this was a good idea. I don't even know this man. But I'm desperate.

ARTHUR: This is a medicine with twelve plants in it. It's called... pandemic medicine. It'll help you. Have some. I'll call in the healing spirits....

ALICE: God, I have so much going on. So many things to do…

The man (BEN) awakens.

BEN: Something is happening…

ALICE: I do so much on my own, now this?

BEN: I'm awake…

ALICE: I don't know what to do. Dad…

BEN: This doesn't feel like healing.

ALICE: All this silence and seriousness is so awkward. It's taking a long time.

BEN: Hurts to talk.

ALICE: Maybe I should've just taken you back to the hospital. But it's so expensive. God, I hate doing all this on my own…

BEN: I had that nightmare. Walking along a gravel road, and a dark shadow in the bush staring at me, following me. I was always scared. But after fear comes anger. Now in my dreams, I yell and swear at the dark shadow. So don't worry, I'm not scared anymore, my girl. I got you back. I'm happy.

ALICE: What am I gonna do? How much did I pay this guy? This doesn't feel right. How are you really doing, Dad? You don't look good…

BEN: I never heard of this man, though. Why does he have pandemic medicine? Is it real? I guess it doesn't matter. I'm not scared, my girl…

ALICE: What's his name again? Great Wind Man?

BEN: *…so cold…*

…hurts…

…can't breathe…

ALICE: Please make him better. Please…

BEN closes his eyes. The elder prays silently. They all exit.

Beat.

Guitar and vocal chorus fade.

DARREN: That's it?

MADGE: That's it. And here that man ended up passing away. The next night.

DARREN: Geez.

MADGE: They didn't find that elder, either.

DARREN: Was it a Native guy?

MADGE: I think so. But no one even talked about it for the longest time. So there's nothing really known beyond that. Maybe let's not talk about it anymore. I'm sorry I brought it up. Makes me mad and I don't feel like getting worked up before a feast.

DARREN: All right.

MADGE: Thank you. So what are you up to now, Darren?

DARREN: Getting ready for work.

MADGE: Work? Good. That's good. Doing what?

DARREN: I'm supposed to be starting on Monday. Paved road project.

MADGE: Paved road? *Wacistakats*, you didn't hear yet.

DARREN: What?

MADGE: They have to cancel.

DARREN: WHAT!? They're cancelling?!

MADGE: Yeah. They don't have the money.

WALLY enters with a small blanket.

WALLY: Here ya go, Madge. Straight from the dollar store. Ahem. Five bucks that blanket. Yup. So, uh –

Holds his hand out. MADGE shakes it.

MADGE: That's your treaty money right there. Well spent. *Miywasin.* Okay, gotta go. *Mwestas.* (Later.)

WALLY: Uh, yup. Have a good day, Madge. *Mwestas.*

DARREN: See ya.

MADGE exits.

Fuck sakes! FUCK! Damn chief! What the hell?! What am I gonna do? I needed that job! FUCK!

WALLY: Please don't swear.

DARREN: Damn Brad! He said I was in! He told me I was in!

WALLY: Don't go getting all worked up. You'll find work.

DARREN: Find work?! When they need security at the Stone Pipe Pow Wow? I can't wait 'til next summer. You don't get it. I need a job now. That's how I got parole. I gotta report next week!

WALLY: I know. I know. Just relax.

DARREN: What am I gonna do!?

WALLY: When's the last time you went to sweat?

DARREN: That's the last thing that's gonna help. I need more than prayers and perspiration! Shit!

WALLY: Darren.

DARREN: What?

WALLY: Don't swear.

DARREN: Yeah, well, you're not the one that's screwed here!

Pause.

I'm sorry. I'm sorry. I'm just...I'm in a really tough spot. You're right. I have no business swearing around. Especially since you're putting me up. I hate this. Who the hell is going to hire a fucking...sorry, shit, sorry...jailbird? UGH!

WALLY grabs the pan.

WALLY: *Astam. Api ōta.* (Come. Sit here.)

DARREN: What?

DARREN sits as WALLY grabs the pan.

WALLY: *Tanisi kīya nikosis?* (How are you, my son?)

DARREN: Shitty. Sorry. I mean crappy.

WALLY: Nothing a good smudge doesn't fix. You need to be clean four days, though, in order to smudge, so...

DARREN: Really? One sip of beer?

WALLY: I'll smudge for you.

DARREN: Whatever.

WALLY says a quiet prayer.

WALLY: *Hei hei.* That's how we say thank you. *Hei hei.*

DARREN: Yeah, well, it's gonna be "bye-bye" for Darren.

WALLY: Let's talk.

DARREN: I don't wanna talk right now. I need a job. Brad said I was in –

WALLY: Never mind your cousin. Can't count on that one. Know why? He talks out of his ass.

DARREN: Great.

Pause.

At least Brad called and came to visit. How come you never did?

WALLY: When? Oh, you mean when you were in the pen?

DARREN: Yeah. Two and a half years, you could have visited.

WALLY: Wanna hear a story?

DARREN: No.

WALLY: Aw, come on. You used to like my stories. In Cree we say *mētoni kayas.* A long time ago.

DARREN: Hurry up…

WALLY: I was in the city, with an old buddy…

Enter ARTHUR with beer.

We were sitting in that old bar that's not there anymore. Figured we'd pick up drinks for the road. Arthur bought. Went out to take a piss in the alley. Arthur's truck was out front. Then two cops come around the corner…

KELLY and HEATHER enter.

KELLY: Good evening, fellas. Uh, sir? I'm sorry, but you can't urinate out here.

ARTHUR: Uh oh. Wally.

WALLY: Uh?

KELLY: You can't urinate out here, sir.

HEATHER: *(Sighs.)* Of course. Drunk Indians. Embarrassing.

ARTHUR: Uh, think I'll just go inside there, buddy. Good night, ladies.

KELLY: Sir? One second.

WALLY: Come on. I'm not bothering anyone.

KELLY: Yes, but still, you can't. They have washrooms inside.

HEATHER: This isn't the rez.

WALLY: And what would you two know about the rez, *picikwāsak?* (apples?)

ARTHUR zips up.

KELLY: Sir.

ARTHUR: *Picikwās!*

KELLY: Okay, that's enough.

ARTHUR: *Picikwās.*

HEATHER: SCREW YOU!

KELLY: Okay, Heather –

HEATHER: Wait, Kelly. You know? We see people like you all the time. Our own people. Weak. Lost. But also irresponsible and in denial.

ARTHUR: I have to go, Wally Marten. Bye.

ARTHUR exits quickly.

KELLY: Sir? Sir.

KELLY exits. HEATHER steps in closer to WALLY.

HEATHER: We're not apples. We're Cree women.

Pause.

I grew up on the reserve, okay? Broken home, just like the rest. Mom at home. Dad gone.

Pause. She leans in, her hand unclipping her gun holster. Calm and collected.

My dad worked hard. Kept us together. Not like you. Indian men like you are embarrassing. To all our people.

WALLY: Is that so?

HEATHER: Bums who fool themselves into believing they're mean and tough. It's all they got. Delusion. All you got. Think you're a tough guy or what?

WALLY: What'd you call me?

HEATHER: Are you a tough guy?

WALLY: *Kikwaya?* (What?)

HEATHER: What?

WALLY: Did you just call me a *taguy?* (penis?)

HEATHER: A what? I said a tough –

WALLY: *"Ta-guy"?* You called me a *taguy.*

HEATHER: Wh – No I –

WALLY: Call me a *taguy?* Your elder? NO RESPECT.

HEATHER: What the hell are you –

WALLY turns HEATHER around and gives her one good spank, while managing to grab her gun.

WALLY: Never mind! Look here, THIS OLD *taguy* just grabbed your gun. HA!

HEATHER is still.

Nech. You feel lucky or what? Now get the hell out of here.

HEATHER exits. WALLY puts the gun in the garbage.

Good thing I finished taking a piss. Never mind, I think I shit my pants.

DARREN: You're a f – what the – Man, you need help. Did that really happen? No. When did this – You know, if you really did that, you'd be in a lot of trouble –

WALLY: Hey. Come on. It's just a story…

DARREN: This is why you didn't visit me? You're so full of it. Just be honest, you know. That's all I ask.

WALLY: You were almost smiling when I said *taguy* –

DARREN: Stop!

WALLY: Okay…just that I haven't seen you smile in a while…

Awkward moment.

DARREN: Whatever. How come you never called, at least? You have a landline.

WALLY: Not long distance. Not on a waterman's salary. I got one now, though. Got this fancy one when I had my money. Fancy one. If you were in jail now I'd be able to call. If I had minutes…

DARREN: Do they even make Blackberry anymore?

WALLY: Chokecherry, I call it. Just a real rez phone.

DARREN: And now that your settlement money's gone you expect to keep up payments on two phones? 'Cuz you're still on a waterman's salary.

WALLY: Nah. Probably won't. You ever wonder why us Indians don't pay our cellphone bills? We're just being tradish. Jumping month to month, contract to contract, phone to phone. It's that semi-nomadic instinct kicking in.

DARREN: What am I going to do?

WALLY: Oh, come now, son. Hey. I got something to show you. *Ceskwa.* (Wait.) Be right back. Don't go anywhere, okay?

WALLY exits.

DARREN: We're on the reserve. Nearest house is two kilometres away. Where am I gonna go?

WALLY: *(From offstage.)* You should think about moving to the city once your parole is up. More work out there.

DARREN: The city's always been a problem for me. Just 'cuz you're broke doesn't mean you can't get into trouble.

WALLY: You should be closer. Closer to your son, I mean. They have places you can stay, don't they?

DARREN: Sally Ann's? You think I wanna share space with a bunch of guys?

WALLY: The pen, though – never mind. But what if you did get a job before Monday? You'd be good, right?

DARREN: I'm a Native man who's spent too much time behind bars. The only references I have, I've beaten up. Who's going to hire me?

WALLY: You'd be surprised.

DARREN: I'm not working where I'm a raisin in rice pudding, which is most places. I'm too smart for SARCAN. I'm too young for Wal-Mart and I'm too old to start over. At my age, I should have my own place, job, a vehicle and be taking care of my son.

WALLY enters with an old guitar.

WALLY: Remember how to play this?

DARREN: You still play?

WALLY: Picked it up when I went on a trip to Chiapas. *Mahalo* (Thank you)...cheap and ugly, but still.

DARREN: What?

WALLY: And I thought I was deaf. *MA-HA-LO...*

DARREN: No, I meant your trip – never mind. *Mahalo?*

WALLY: Aha. *Mahalo. Tapwe.*

DARREN: Chiapas?

WALLY: I know, hey? Musta borrowed it from them Hawaiians. Nice, huh? In Mexico it was on sale for two hundred and seventy-five pesos at the time. Two hundred and seventy-five?! I was gonna shit myself. Then I learned how much that was in Canadian and didn't end up shitting myself.

No comment from DARREN.

But go on. Play it! I know you still got it in you. Play some Bob Seger.

DARREN: No.

WALLY: Be fun. You used to love jamming. Used to play for me and my buddy.

DARREN: Your buddy? That same one from "the bar that's not there anymore" story?

WALLY: He ditched. That's the point. Said my name, too. *Taguy.* Man, I was stupid. But then again I was young.

DARREN: Now you're just old.

WALLY: What?

DARREN: The Wally I know would've beat the shit out of him. That's all.

WALLY: Language, Darren. I used to be like that…violent… messed up. Not anymore. I'm healed now.

DARREN: So you ARE just too old then?

WALLY: Look who's talking? Thirty around the corner.

DARREN: I'm thirty-one.

WALLY: Things change in your thirties. And hey. My last name might be Marten but at one time I was a grizzly. *Metoni kayas.* This is one of my best stories. One time, I kicked a guy's ass…just for you…

Lights, music. Enter ARTHUR with alcohol. He sits beside WALLY, who is ready to sing a song. They are drunk.

'Kay then, 'kay then. Hey, hey, buddy.

ARTHUR: Hey. Play a song there, Wally.

WALLY: Hey, hey…buddy…look at this picture. This is my – my boy there, Darren. Hey, my boy?

ARTHUR: Heyyy. All right, Darwin –

WALLY: Darren, I said.

ARTHUR: Oh. Sorry. Sorry. Play some Bob Seger, there, Wally.

WALLY: Hey, buddy. Hey, how come you ditched me?

ARTHUR: What're you talking about?

WALLY: You ditched me.

ARTHUR: I'm not ditching you. Come on, sing. We need more beers. Sing Bob Seger 'til a ride gets here.

WALLY: *Namoya.* (No.) I'll sing for my boy. This is my boy's favourite song. It's a song I wrote for Darren.

ARTHUR: Okay, then. All right. But play some Bob Seger after, okay, Wally?

WALLY: *Namoya.* (No.) I'll sing Hank. Or Johnny.

ARTHUR: This guy. Come on, sing something! It'll take a while for my buddy to get here. SING!

WALLY: Okay, I'll sing you my boy's favourite song. A song I wrote. For my boy.

Kisses the picture.

Buddy, hey, buddy, goes like this…hey, my boy? Listen and learn. *(WALLY sings.)*

Well, it's the same
Oh, it's the same
It's all the same how we play
This game

Well, it's all talk
Oh, it's all talk
It's all talk so I think
I'll just walk…

ARTHUR: Heyyy. Allriight. Good song. Cheers.

WALLY: *So just hold out your hand*
From where you stand
So take a little chance
And let's dance, dance, dance

Wooooooo!

ARTHUR: Good song. Holeh. Cheers again.

WALLY: Hey, my boy? Buddy…this is my boy.

ARTHUR: Cheers, Damien…

WALLY: NO! No…I told you – Darren! Fuck, I told you Darren!

ARTHUR: Heyyy. *Niciwakan ekosi* there, holy. (That's it, my friend.)

WALLY: FUCK YOU! I told you Darren twice already! Teach you to forget my boy's name! Never mind sorry! Asshole!

WALLY hits ARTHUR.

ARTHUR: Heyyyy –

WALLY: Shut up! Damn guy, you –

WALLY hits ARTHUR again. The hits are violent until WALLY throws him to one end of the room, where ARTHUR lies motionless, then stands and exits.

Damn guy! Asshole…ditched me again.

WALLY takes a seat and sips on water. DARREN stares.

DARREN: Sometimes you just go too far with your stories.

WALLY: Sure. Ask your m – uh, your uncles. Ah, never mind, they were all too drunk to remember anything. Was…at Auntie Gina's, I think.

DARREN: Auntie Gina's? Which time? Did that really happen? Who was it?

WALLY: Huh?

DARREN: Who was the guy?

WALLY: What?

DARREN: The guy.

WALLY: *Taguy?* Who's a *taguy?* Oh, the guy! I told you…

DARREN: No, you didn't.

WALLY: What?

DARREN: Nothing, I just – holy, never mind. Nothing.

Silence. WALLY plays the guitar.

WALLY: *(Sings.)*

Well, it's the same
Oh…how we play this game

He stops.

It's a story…with a point. And the point is I'm not like that anymore. Healed…

DARREN: I hate it when you do that.

WALLY: Haven't played that song in a long time. I can't remember the words. Wanna play?

DARREN: No.

WALLY: Come on.

DARREN: No. Look, Wally, stop. Okay?

WALLY: Just to get your mind off –

DARREN: HOLY CHRIST, YOU DON'T LISTEN. Okay. What THEN? What do you got? Do you have a job for me? Huh, WALLY? No? Okay then. Stop with the guitar and trying to make me feel better!

Pause.

I –...sorr – Man. Shit. I don't mean to be like this. Really. I just don't know what I'm gonna do. I can't go back.

WALLY: I know.

WALLY refers to the newspaper.

Know what we need? A plan. Let's think about what's going on. Fall means harvest, people getting engaged after a *nicimos* (my sweetheart) summer... Oh...school year's just started up. Look! They're hiring. I can apply for a different job. A better paying job. *Soniyaw* (money) from the *moniyaw (*white man). Real *soniyaw*. Save and help you out. Eh?

DARREN: You can't be a teacher.

WALLY: No, I mean they're looking for an elder.

DARREN chokes on his drink.

DARREN: Elder? You? Elder?

WALLY: Yeah.

DARREN: We'd have better luck if I ran for chief. And that isn't saying much.

WALLY: I could be an elder. Do it for me and you and Michel. Family. If I got this job, you can take over my shifts and –

DARREN: Are you saying I should follow in your footsteps and be the next waterman!?

WALLY: Yeah. Keep you out of jail, anyways.

DARREN: I don't even have a driver's licence!

WALLY: Pfft. Neither do I. That's the best thing about driving on the reserve. Especially a band vehicle. They don't care. RCs never stop you anyways. It's water!! Plus no one with a driver's licence wants this job. Triple-bogey!

DARREN: Do you even know what a triple bo – never mind.

WALLY: Plus, if I make elder, it'll look good for you. Come on, I got a pretty good look for the job, eh?

No reply from DARREN.

It's all set then. I'm goin' to the band office –

DARREN: The school.

WALLY: To the school, and I'm gonna apply for that job! Help my son…and my grandson in the progress.

DARREN: Process.

WALLY: Yes! No. Or wait. Huh?

DARREN: What?

WALLY: Yes.

DARREN: This is a bad idea.

WALLY: Yup. And after I'll make us some rabbit soup for supper! *Waposomīcimapoy.* (Rabbit soup.) To celebrate. Cool, man. I'm going to be Stone Pipe's next elder. About time, too.

DARREN: You gotta be damn kidding.

WALLY: Damn rights! *Ekwa maka.* (Let's go.)

DARREN: Now?

WALLY: Yes, now! To change the future! Change it now. Holy. *(Takes a deep breath.)* I can just imagine my first public speech…

Spotlight comes up on a podium.

Tānisi kahkiyaw kīyawaw? (Hello all, how are you?) *Kinanaskōmitinawāw napewak ekwa iskwewak.* (Thank you, ladies and gentlemen.) *Wally Marten nitsiyihkason ekwa nīya ohci asini-ospwakanihk ōta.* (My name is Wally Marten and I'm from Stone Pipe.) Wally Marten: Elder. From here on in, everyone's gonna call me…*mosōm* (grandfather). Yeah, I got this.

Ekwa maka. (Let's go.)

DARREN: Fuck.

They exit.

Scene 2

A hallway. DARREN and WALLY find themselves outside the principal's office. Classes are in session.

DARREN: Wally, I don't think this is a good idea.

WALLY: What's this principal's name again?

DARREN: Don't know.

WALLY: I wonder where she's from.

WALLY peers into her office.

DARREN: She's new. Never met her. Look, I think we can figure something else out –

WALLY: Oh great. She's *moniyaw iskwew.* (white woman.)

DARREN: So she's white. So what?

WALLY: Son. There are some people in this world. They just don't know. They don't understand. They think they know and they push to make "improvements." Most of the time they just make things worse. It worries me. I hope this woman is not like that.

No reply from DARREN.

You think she's shacked up here?

DARREN: I doubt it. We would've heard if she was.

WALLY: Too bad. Too many cousins on the rez getting married and whatnot. I wonder why she'd wanna work on the rez.

DARREN: We're an hour from the city. Not much of a commute.

WALLY: Commute. Second time I heard that word today. Your cousin Brad was using it to try sound fancy and stuff. And here he's never even left the reserve. Hmm, she's busy. I guess we just wait 'til this woman gets off the phone. Don't talk to any kids, might be yours. Just kidding. Did I ever teach you how to do a reserve Windsor?

DARREN: What's a reserve Windsor?

WALLY: Only the luckiest tie ever. Puts the short end in the front. À la, backwards. Watch and learn.

DARREN: Do you mean reverse Windsor?

WALLY: No. Holy. Reserve Windsor! Only works if you're Indian…on white people…on the reserve. Makes them wanna correct you and feel good about themselves or something.

DARREN: Geez.

WALLY: We need all the luck we can get if we're gonna get you back on your feet and that crazy half-breed-speaking woman off your back. Does she speak half?

DARREN: Easy, geez! It's Michif. That's what they speak.

WALLY: Ch, how do you know?

DARREN: Madge.

WALLY: Michif. Right, like how we say *nehiyawewin.* (Cree language.)

DARREN: Yeah.

WALLY: Cool. Hey, how come you never finished high school?

DARREN: Are you kidding? Old St. Philip's? The residential school? C'mon. You don't remember? Mom decided I should go live with *kohkom* (grandmother) and *mosom* (grandfather) in the city.

WALLY: Oh yeah. I wish this high school was here at the time. You could've gotten your grade twelve. Maybe go to university. Met a smart *nehiyaw* (Cree) woman.

DARREN: I don't think so.

WALLY: Instead of that Michif-speaking half-breed.

DARREN: Hey!

WALLY: Well, I just know them…Métis.

DARREN: Like who? You don't know any, except Cindy. And barely.

WALLY: One bad bannock moulds the rest, am I right?

DARREN has no words.

It's just – she seems to give you such a hard time, though.

DARREN: They probably say the same about us.

WALLY: *Ekosi anima.* (That is it.) The reserve Windsor. You like the tie? Picked it up in a Chiapas market.

DARREN: Yeah, it's nice.

WALLY: You know them Indians in Mexico sell their stuff right on the street. Food, blankets, clothing. Don't even charge tax or nothing. No tax? That's the world I wanna live in.

DARREN: Good luck. Listen, this isn't gonna work so I'm just gonna –

WALLY: Hey. There's that feast this afternoon! The one Madge talked about. In the gym.

Pause.

DARREN: No.

WALLY: *Kihkway?* (What?)

DARREN: I'm not going.

WALLY: Oh, come on. It'll be good. Pray to the grandfathers and grandmothers. *Kahkiyaw niwakomakanak.* All my relations. Eat some good food and visit. Might be a good way to get a foot in the door.

DARREN: How many elders do we have on the reserve?

WALLY: Well, there's ole Barbie Barbara, Slim Jim, Big Grant, Big Mouth Madge, Gumboot Gary, Lucky Leroy, Backroad Matt…

DARREN: There ya go. And they're all more qualified than you. So don't go counting your –

WALLY: You're right. Most of them sweat every Sunday out at Backroad's lodge. Come with me to the feast.

DARREN: Why?

WALLY: They'll all be there, I bet. I need the inside scoop on who's going for that job. Need a wingman.

DARREN: Do you even know what a wing – I told you I don't wanna go. I don't do feasts anymore.

WALLY: Why not?

DARREN: I always get asked to serve. I hate serving. My back acts up. No one looks me in the eye. Like I'm too scary. It's embarrassing. And what's up with the lard at feasts? You know that tablespoonful they make everyone swallow before we're actually allowed to eat?

WALLY: It's the way we do it. Darren –

DARREN: Really? Who's "we"? Stone Pipe Indians? Plains Cree People? Aboriginal Canadians? Better not over-generalize, there, Wally. Someone might take advantage and try sell ceremonial lard.

WALLY: It's not the same everywhere –

DARREN: And all on the same spoon. Not very sanitary, you think?

WALLY: You're getting carried away.

DARREN: Plus, all the food's mixed together. Not a far cry from jail food.

WALLY: Hey! That's enough! What's wrong with you? Holy. Okay, she's off the phone. Here I go…

WALLY closes his eyes and takes a deep breath.

Ekwa e-waskweyawin. And he becomes part of his destiny.

DARREN: You sound like *Star Wars*.

WALLY: Change, like a change in the wind, is coming soon. And *mosom* here thinks it's about friggin' time.

DARREN: God help us all.

WALLY: At least say Creator, son. Creator help us all. God sounds too churchy…

DARREN: Good luck.

WALLY: Thanks.

DARREN: No, really. Good luck. I'll be outside.

WALLY: *Ekwa maka…*

They take separate exits.

Scene 3

It is later that afternoon. DARREN arrives back at the house. He grabs a beer and sits to watch TV. The phone rings.

DARREN: Hello?

Ugh.

Really?

Incoherent yelling.

You know you have the worst timing ever?... No. I haven't found – they cancelled...This is the reserve. It's going to take time...Of course, I'm looking...I know...Yeah...Yeah...Yeah...Holy shit, were you this bitchy and demanding when we were together? Pfft...yeah, right...as if... Don't phone here again, Cindy. I won't answer!

He hangs up. WALLY enters with food from the feast, all in Tupperware.

WALLY: Score! Son, I got some soup, bannock and wild meat. Treats, too. Holeh, now, that was a good feast. Been a while since I smoked the pipe with the elders. *Miywasin,* boy. Good medicine. Next time you should come. You'll like it. I got a new job coming up and we'll be busy on the good red road.

DARREN: You got the job!?

WALLY: Yes! *(Pause.)* And no.

DARREN: What does that mean?

WALLY: Well, no because they have to complete interviews first. And yes because the deadline's Monday and no one applied but me!

DARREN: No one's applying?

WALLY: Everyone's either busy or staying at home enjoying their pension. Hehe. I'm shoed-in. See? The reserve Windsor. How did you get back?

DARREN: I got a ride with the garbage man.

WALLY: Been doing that job forever. Good man, that one. Doesn't have his driver's either. So…you just…

DARREN: I didn't ditch. You saw me wave at the door when I was leaving.

WALLY: Thought you were cheering me on. Oh, well. So hey, guess what? I'm gonna build a sweat lodge.

DARREN: What?!

WALLY: Well, not all of it. Just the frame. Remember? Madge gave me the tobacco. Gotta do it.

DARREN: Oh, yeah.

WALLY: Don't worry, though. Madge already did the prep work. Did the prayer, songs, offerings and all.

DARREN: Oh, yeah.

WALLY: Yeah. So all that's gotta be done is the wood, rocks. Put the willow in, tobacco down, prayers and tie 'em up. *Tapwe.* Easy, huh?

DARREN: Yeah, easy.

Pause.

No.

WALLY: Huh?

DARREN: No, I said.

WALLY: No? No what?

DARREN: I'm not going.

WALLY: Really?

DARREN: Really. NO!

WALLY: Oh...okay, son. I understand. Sounds good. Wellll, gotta be up early. Better crash. My arthritis is worse these days, so gotta get more rest. I was hoping to take up running, you know... jogging? But my knees...*oweya* (an expression of surprise)...just squeaky. The hips too just act up all the time. You don't have Tylenol? No or yes? Ah, that's okay. I'll be good. *Oweya*...

DARREN: I'll help next time.

WALLY: Uh huh, *tapwe. Miywasin, nikōsis.* (Good, son.) Hey. Did I ever tell you? One thing about being old is, time sure goes by. Like fast, too. *Sēmak.* (Hurry.) Holy. I sure hope those – nah, I'll be okay out there by myself. Coyotes probably went south already...Can't wait to see my grandson... after all, that's who I'm doing this all for...

DARREN: Ah, shit. All right, all right. I'll help!

WALLY: Right on, son. Love you. Be ready to go by four-thirty.

DARREN: In the afternoon. Got it.

WALLY: Morning. We gotta make sure the door is facing true east when the sun first shines.

DARREN: Dammit...

WALLY approaches DARREN.

WALLY: Wow. We're gonna build a sweat lodge. You're a good son. See you in the morning...

DARREN: Fuck...

They take separate exits.

END of ACT I

ACT II

Scene 1

WALLY and DARREN are out in a clearing. WALLY is taking his time.

WALLY: Hm. Yup, this is the spot. True east. Let's get started.

DARREN: It's cold out.

WALLY: Of course; it's October. *Pimihāwi-pīsim,* the migrating moon. Grab the hatchet in the truck.

DARREN exits while WALLY begins.

Bring my gloves, too.

DARREN: Yeah, I got 'em.

WALLY: Right on. Okay…

WALLY makes an offering. (The building of the lodge should be abstract, created using a movement coach or choreographer in consultation with an elder.)

Hei hei.

DARREN: I haven't seen the morning star in a long time.

WALLY: Yeah, remember when you, me and your mom used to come make fires on the other side of that bush there?

DARREN: I don't wanna talk about it.

WALLY: Just saying. You know, me, you and Michel can come out here. Look at the sky. Stars.

DARREN: How long is this gonna take? Jets are playing the Flames this afternoon and I wanna get some more sleep before it's on.

WALLY: Ah, never mind. Your *mosom* watched that and wrestling when he should have been building lodges of his own.

DARREN: Don't talk about my mom's dad, okay?

WALLY: I'm just saying. If he followed the culture the way he followed hockey, he would have passed it on to you – That's what I wanna do for my grandson.

DARREN: Okay, that's enough.

WALLY: Okay.

Pause. WALLY continues the frame.

Are you gonna come sweat when this is up?

DARREN: No.

WALLY: Why not?

DARREN: Not ready. Plus, I'm not interested.

WALLY: *Awas.* Any time's a good time to sweat.

DARREN: Doesn't matter if culture is on the inside. Jail does nothing but educate criminals.

WALLY: Is that what you think you are?

DARREN: Maybe. I know that's how everyone sees me. My PO, the reserve, Cindy, you.

WALLY: Ah! *Mahti maka nikosis.* (That's enough, son.)

DARREN: I know it's true.

WALLY: I don't. I don't see you that way. That's ridiculous.

DARREN: Really? What do you see then?

WALLY: I see an angry man. Frustrated and hurting. Unable to handle how he feels about life.

DARREN: Oh, crap. Here it comes…

WALLY: You just gotta believe, son. And smudge. Believe those ancestors will hear your prayers and help you.

DARREN: I prayed once, in jail…for a friend of mine. Small, skinny, weak. Did he ever get it. I prayed he would be okay so he could get out and be with anyone on the outside who cared for him.

In the end, he couldn't handle it. Hung himself, with a shoestring.

I've prayed many times in my life, actually, if you need to know. Many times…and nothing's gotten – I don't know if I've given up or am hopelessly waiting…I don't know…but it feels like the more the days go by, the less I care…

WALLY: When I went down to Chiapas, we went to this sacred gathering…of Indians from all over the world. It was called "The Beginning of Change and the New Dawn." A sacred four-day gathering. Home of the ancestors from down south. And you know what? They paid for everyone to go there. Put them up. Fed them. And the message we all came out with was "To return to our traditional ways of knowing and living."

DARREN: What? Wait. Hold on. Back up. You got a free plane ride, hotel and meals to learn that we should return to our old ways?

WALLY: Well, not me. Just the people invited. I paid for my own way.

DARREN: Wally, are you kidding me? To learn a message we've been saying since contact? What the hell? What a waste!

WALLY: What is wrong with you? You don't understand. There were spiritual medicine men from all over the world. Men that could read you like a picture book, boy! Don't judge, either. You still drink! Even on parole. You're lucky I don't –

DARREN: I don't drink to get drunk. That's the difference between you and me. I have a few times. Who doesn't? But I've never hurt anyone, woken up in jail, spent all my money or broke the law because of alcohol. I ended up behind bars because of what I learned from you. Anger and violence. Don't need alcohol for that. And before you judge, think about this: sobriety is for the weak. They have to be sober. Because they have no control, no sense of responsibility, no control of anything. They can't handle their alcohol. Like you.

WALLY stops bending the willow.

WALLY: I don't have to listen to this. You know what? Ever since you first went to jail, you've had this shitty disrespectful attitude. You stopped believing in anything. And ever since you stopped believing, your life's been getting worse. I can do this on my own. Why don't you go sit in the truck?

DARREN: Nah, I'll just walk.

WALLY: What is this? Why are you being like this?! You never acted like this when your mom was around. She would be –

DARREN: Oh shut up. Do you ever shut the hell up, Wally? You always gotta play the "mom" card?

WALLY: Just saying…

DARREN: You wanna know? Do you? Mr. Born-Again Indian?!

WALLY: Enough, you little –

DARREN: Get your fucking hands off me!

WALLY: Just tell me, dammit! I can still kick your ass, then have you sent right back to jail!

DARREN: Nice to see you again, Dad.

WALLY sits, stunned. Enter ARTHUR with his suitcase. Two women enter and take their seat, in gowns.

ARTHUR: *Ahaw. Nanaskimonawaw, nosimak* for coming. (Thanks, my grandchildren.) *Kahkiyaw mina tawaw.* (Welcome.)

DARREN: You know, I used to really feel good about who I was – Remember when you took me to that asshole's sweat lodge after Mom died? Huh?

WALLY: Darren, this isn't –

DARREN: But he had one of them Hollywood Indian names at the time.

WALLY: Well, he is Cree.

DARREN: Right…I forgot, he is a Cree Indian. Called himself Broken Wind or some shit…

ARTHUR: *Ahaw.*

DARREN: Where's my dad?

ARTHUR: CLOSE THE DOOR, *oskapew.* (helper.) Shh. Thank you all for coming. Welcome. My Indian name is Wind Spirit Man and – hey. No. Not like that, like this. See? Good. Good boy, this one. Smart. Should make a good husband and father someday. Make sure, ladies, your daughters snag him now. Heyyyyy.

DARREN: But am I really going to talk with my mom?

ARTHUR: Yes, your mom and the spirits will reach out to you in my lodge today.

DARREN: The door closes and its dark. Anyway, we all take our place. This medicine man friend of yours starts singing.

ARTHUR: Pray, everyone.

DARREN: So everyone starts whispering some prayers. And we hear it. His rattle.

ARTHUR: My people. Thank you for inviting us the grandfather spirits into your lodge. I'm the spirit of the crow. Do you want to see me?

DARREN: So he starts shaking his rattle and in an instant there it is. The sparks on the ground. Blue sparks.

WALLY: So?

DARREN: The rocks were flint, Wally. And he probably had some bits of iron in it, too. They were flint rocks in his rattle! When flint makes contact with iron it causes a spark! If you'd made it to Grade Eight you'd know that.

WALLY: Stop.

Rattle stops.

ARTHUR: Ten splashes.

WALLY: You're crossing the line –

DARREN: Who the hell splashes that many times? So about three minutes later, the door opens. Everyone lies on the ground, gasping and overheated.

ARTHUR: Don't lie on your back, my people.

WALLY: It lets bad spirits in, that's why.

DARREN: YEAH, I KNOW. Second round. Door closes. A drum beats…water is splashed on the rocks again…everyone prays…I don't. I hear him humming or something…I don't know…a song follows…

ARTHUR: *Ahaw.* Time to invite the spirits of all directions to watch over us during this holy sweat lodge. The sound of the drum is a stampede for healing, from the spirits of Grandmother and Grandfather Buffalo. We are thankful. *Ahaw.* Okay, pray. Pray, all of you…

DARREN: The voices are louder…drum, too…Arthur's singing…

Sound of a rattle.

I hear a rattle…Everyone's praying…except me…and in all of that…it suddenly became silent.

Silence.

Mom?

Pause.

Then I feel it.

WALLY: What?

DARREN: Arthur. His hand. On my leg. Touching me…

Pause.

Son of a bitch. Wanna hear the rest? No? Didn't think so. Just when I believed I was going to get to speak with Mom one last time.

WALLY: Oh, Darren…

By this point the skeleton of the lodge is almost done, except for the willow branches that each hold.

DARREN: And where were you? Outside, being the helper. After Mom died you were so depressed. Absent. But finally happy to be doing something… helpful. So I never said anything.

WALLY: Darren…

DARREN: So yeah. There ya go! That's why I "lost my faith"! Now you know why I hate everything to do with culture, with language, with ceremony!

Pause.

I'm walking back to the house.

DARREN exits. WALLY stands alone.

Scene 2

Sound of a truck that won't start. DARREN is taking a leak off a dark road on the north end of the reserve.

WALLY: *Ceskwa.* (Wait.) Hey, wait up.

DARREN: What?

WALLY: Truck's outta gas. I'll walk with you. *Ceskwa,* gotta pee.

DARREN: You finished?

WALLY: Door's true east, that's what counts. Pit, wood and rocks are next. Pretty cold, so I'll have to wait 'til the ground's softer anyways. I'll get a few hours rest then come back and finish up. The truck will be safe.

DARREN: Got any tobacco left?

WALLY: Offering's not gonna do anything. Outta gas. We just gotta keep waiting. Don't worry. I forgot about those rabbits. I'll cook up some soup when we get back.

DARREN: I just wanted to roll a smoke.

WALLY: Thought you quit.

DARREN: Don't start…

WALLY: Smoking's not good for you. Wasn't good for your mom.

DARREN: Okay, stop.

WALLY: Okay. Just saying. What are you doing with papers?

DARREN: Brad.

WALLY: Of course.

DARREN: What's that?

WALLY: What? Where?

DARREN: There? Someone's walking. Who's that?

WALLY: Where? I can't see –

DARREN: There. On the right side of the road.

WALLY: Oh. I don't know.

DARREN: Hitchhiker?

WALLY: Looks like…

Enter ARTHUR. He startles DARREN and WALLY.

ARTHUR: HELLO. Ooops. Didn't mean to startle youse.

DARREN: Geez.

WALLY: Well, you did.

ARTHUR: My car ran out of gas just out of town. Gas station's closed so I decided to –

WALLY: Arthur…

DARREN and WALLY freeze.

ARTHUR: Heyyy. Wally. Holy.

WALLY: What are you doing here?

ARTHUR: Wally Marten. Hehe. Quite the run-in, eh? I haven't even been here a minute and already I run into Wally Marten. Hehe.

WALLY: Where did you come from?

ARTHUR: Regina. City that rhymes with fun.

DARREN: Gawd. You're still such a –

Car horn and lights. DARREN stops.

ARTHUR: Oh. Right on, boy! Hey, it's a truck, too. Hey, we should ride in the back. Like old times. Hey, Wally?

WALLY: No. We'll pass. UH, THANKS, BUT WE'LL PASS.

ARTHUR: You sure? Okay. Heyyy. We should catch up. I'm looking for a job. Lunch in town tomorrow, Wally? We got some things to talk about. Important things. Just me and you. I'll buy. Later, boys.

Sound of a truck door opening and closing. Incoherent discussion. The truck drives off.

DARREN: WHAT THE HELL?!

WALLY: What could he possibly want?

DARREN: Don't tell me you're going.

WALLY: Let's just keep walking, Darren. I gotta let Madge know I finished the frame.

DARREN: Don't tell me.

WALLY: Just never mind, I said! Let's go.

Pause.

DARREN: Wally…

Pause.

How did he even start all his crap?

Scene 3

ARTHUR enters with two of his granddaughters. They are in gowns. He puts down a blanket and a bag. A fire burns with a pile of rocks in the middle.

CHEYENNE: Hey, cousin Serena. Is this *mosom*'s first sweat?

SERENA: Pfft. No. Second.

CHEYENNE: Whoa. Is this your first time?

SERENA: No way. As if, Cheyenne.

CHEYENNE: I heard it's hot.

SERENA: Uh huh, so don't be a big baby now and go crying. Like that time at the pow wow when you peed yourself.

CHEYENNE: No, I didn't.

ARTHUR: Okay. Come in.

SERENA: Let's go. This sweat is for your cousin, hey? 'Cuz she died?

CHEYENNE: Yeah. So…

ARTHUR: Sit on that side, kids. *Ahaw. Tanisi kahkiyaw?* My name is Arthur Bear, but my *Nehiyaw* name is Sacred Wind Man. Pray!

Rattle and drum. The girls speak quietly.

CHEYENNE: It's okay if it's your first time, you know.

SERENA: Who's that man outside? What does he do?

CHEYENNE: See? Told you it's your first time.

Is this gonna be like a sauna?

SERENA: Better than a white man sauna, my *mosom* said. Is this all your family?

CHEYENNE: Yeah, my mom, dad, uncle and auntie.

SERENA: Really? What happened to your cousin?

ARTHUR: Shh. You girls. Pray. I'll throw THIS BRAID OF spiritual MEDICINE on the rocks. Breathe it in!

Everyone coughs. They cough from the dust and heat.

CHEYENNE: What kind of rocks are those?

ARTHUR: Don't ask questions.

SERENA: He doesn't know.

CHEYENNE: Guess not. It's hot in here.

ARTHUR: PRAY. SING. I'LL SPLASH AGAIN. *AHAW.*

CHEYENNE: My dad and mom got into a fight last night.

SERENA: Why?

CHEYENNE: 'Cuz my dad thinks your *mosom* might be a popcorn elder.

SERENA: What's that?

CHEYENNE: It means he's like popcorn.

SERENA: What do you even mean, Cheyenne?

ARTHUR: SHH.

Rattle, drum, prayer and singing are louder.

CHEYENNE: You know. Like instant. Like he's an instant medicine man.

SERENA: Shut up!! SO!?

Splash.

CHEYENNE: Whoa. Water splashed on the rocks!

SERENA: Steam, too. Watch this.

CHEYENNE: Watch what? I can't see. Ow!

ARTHUR: *Oweya*. Holy.

CHEYENNE: Ow. *Mosom* Arthur.

SERENA: *Oweya!* Use your towel.

CHEYENNE: It's hot. It hurts.

SERENA: Just lie down.

CHEYENNE: I can't! It hurts! Open the door!

SERENA: OW!

CHEYENNE: OPEN THE DOOR!

ARTHUR: Shit. Uh, WALLY, OPEN THE DOOR.

Awkward silence.

It's okay. Go on. Go in the house.

SERENA: It's too hot. I wanna go, too.

ARTHUR: Yup, okay. It's okay, everyone. Go ahead.

The two girls remove their gowns and exit. WALLY enters.

WALLY: Everything okay?

ARTHUR: Ah, yeah, they just got scared. It's okay, everyone.

WALLY: What now?

ARTHUR: This is not what I thought it would be. I'll do the last two rounds with the rest of the family. Okay, close the door. Okay, everyone, let's pray. *Ahaw…*

Rattle and drum. They take a seat at a table.

Ya, I remember? Why?

WALLY: You burnt that family, including those girls.

ARTHUR: Heyyy. Been over a year. They were okay. Quit being stuck in the past there, Wally! Relax. How are things around here?

WALLY: Like how?

ARTHUR: I don't know. How's everyone?

WALLY: You mean, do people still talk?

ARTHUR: Yeah.

WALLY: Sometimes. Sometimes it's good. Most of the time bad.

ARTHUR: Some things never change.

WALLY: Yeah…

ARTHUR: Yeah…

Pause.

We should go for a drink sometime.

WALLY: I quit.

ARTHUR: What? You? Quit? Since when?

WALLY: Since Chiapas.

ARTHUR: Chiapas? Oh yeah, that Mexico trip. I heard about that. Big Mouth Madge, you know.

Pause.

Why so quiet?

WALLY: I thought you were gone.

ARTHUR: Well, you know…

WALLY: What?

ARTHUR: That was the plan. But…things never work out how you plan.

WALLY: You didn't wanna go live somewhere else?

ARTHUR: Like where? This is my home.

WALLY: Home is where family is. Yours disowned you.

ARTHUR: Pfft.

WALLY: Even your wife's been passed on for years now.

ARTHUR: You're still here. Your woman's been gone many years and your boy was in jail. I haven't seen you go anywhere.

WALLY: Yeah…

ARTHUR: Yeah…

WALLY: Been busy?

ARTHUR: Oh, you know. This and that. Working.

WALLY: Doing what?

ARTHUR: Why you so interested?

WALLY: Not interested, just curious. Same old, I suppose.

ARTHUR: Mm-hm. That your boy that was walking with you last night?

No reply from WALLY.

Same old, yeah. Where nobody knows my name. People are so needy these days for culture and healing. Might as well cash in. Not like I'm the only one doing it, anyway.

WALLY: What? You mean there's a popcorn tribe out there somewhere?

ARTHUR: Eh?

WALLY: How many people have you scammed?

ARTHUR: A lot of white people, they're easy. Can get rich off them, boy. Sick ones. Lost ones. Jailed ones. Even adopted ones. And there so willing to pay money. Is that what you're "curious" about? Money?

WALLY: No.

ARTHUR: Something's different about you, *nīciwakan.* (my friend.)

WALLY: Don't call me friend.

ARTHUR: Easy.

WALLY: We were never friends.

ARTHUR: Wally. The world is messed up. Nothing's real any more. Look at people today. Desperate. These days anyone can take advantage. All you gotta do is speak the language or fake some ceremony or call yourself sober. You see these so-called role models nowadays? "I've had a hard life, but I'm sober now! My life has changed just like that. Your life can too!" and people will follow, even honour them. Pfft, what the hell is that all about?

WALLY: You're sick.

ARTHUR: There's fake people everywhere. First it was them meditation, self-help gurus. Like that *moniyaw* who killed three people in his sweat in Arizona? Well, he's still around. Nothing's real anymore. It's all bullshit.

WALLY: Why do it, then?

ARTHUR: You think I'm the villain? Pfft. They screwed us up. Old St. Philip's. That's why we're all the way we are.

WALLY: That's really getting old, Arthur. The "residential school" card? Why not just claim compensation?

ARTHUR: And forgive? Forgive all that for a measly thirty grand? Like you did?

WALLY: I may have forgiven but I haven't forgotten. I got over it. And I even got a job now.

ARTHUR: You call water delivery a real job? You got it 'cuz no one else wants it. Who the hell would even hire people like us for a real job? This is my form of payback, or is it back pay?

WALLY: Don't touch me!

ARTHUR: Heyyy. Relax.

WALLY: So why come back here? No one wants you here.

ARTHUR: I'm different now.

WALLY: Liar.

DARREN enters, talking on WALLY's cellphone.

DARREN: Yeah, well, I got the steel-toes for nothing then, didn't I, Brad?

Silence. DARREN hangs up.

I thought you were doing the pit, rocks, and wood today.

WALLY: I know, I just needed to –

DARREN: What are you doing here…with him?

WALLY: Son. It's all right. I'll explain later.

DARREN: What the hell?

ARTHUR: Calm yourself. It's a public place.

DARREN: Son of a bitch –

WALLY: Darren –

DARREN: Dead –

A waitress enters.

WAITRESS: Excuse me, is there a problem?

DARREN: Yeah, you've got a pedoph –

WALLY: No.

ARTHUR: No, miss. There's no problem. Just a misunderstanding.

DARREN: To hell with that!

WAITRESS: I'm afraid I'll have to ask you to pay for this now and leave. Sorry.

WALLY: No. Miss, please. Son! WAIT!

ARTHUR: I'll take care of this. My girl, we apologize. This is just a misunderstanding. I'll gladly pay for the meal and here's a ten-dollar tip, if you can just give us a moment. Oh, look, RCs driving by. Wave.

The waitress takes the money and walks away.

As I was saying, I'm different now. I've made some mistakes. And I've had time to think.

DARREN: Bullshit!

WALLY: Darren –

ARTHUR: I just want to stay low and be home. I was born here. I was raised here. I want to be buried here.

WALLY: Why?

ARTHUR: You ask why. I ask why not?

WALLY: But what you've done. It's not right. And not good.

ARTHUR: Oh, like St. Philip's? The way they did to us. To me. Maybe you didn't get felt up and abused, Wally. But I did. I DID!

WALLY: You don't get it. You just don't get it. You can't think there's no consequence.

ARTHUR: I may have done some shit, at least I TRIED to help. Someone out there is better 'cuz of me. And you call it a scam? What about you? Have you helped anyone? Look at your son.

DARREN grabs ARTHUR by the throat.

WALLY: No, son, please! Please! No! Son!

DARREN: You never helped. Not me. Not anyone. Not you. You ruin lives.

He grabs ARTHUR by the shirt and pulls him in.

I promise, there'll be a time when you and I are alone. Fuck people like you!

ARTHUR: People like me. Uh? There's more than just one kind of "person like me." Right, Wally Marten?

WALLY: Shut the hell up.

ARTHUR: Your dad's a good storyteller. *Metoni kayas.* (A very long time ago.) Eh, Wally?

WALLY: Shut up, I said.

ARTHUR: Wally Marten was my *oskapiyew.* Did he ever tell you about being my helper? When you were in the pen? Well, let me tell you how it really happened…

DARREN: What?

ARTHUR: Ya! Just over a year ago. He didn't tell you that story? We got back from a ceremony. Pay day. Picked up some hard stuff. Bugger kept going on about your mom –

Flashback to that night. WALLY and ARTHUR are very intoxicated.

WALLY: …I just miss her, Arthur. I just miss her so much.

ARTHUR: Heyyy. It was a long time ago. *Metoni kayas…*

WALLY: I know. But sometimes I can still see her, hear her, smell her.

ARTHUR: Heyy.

WALLY: Hey…my buddy…thanks for the work, you know? I'm just… I'm pretty messed up right now…

ARTHUR: I know…

WALLY: My boy's in the pen. My boy's gone…

ARTHUR: I know…

WALLY: Thanks for the drinks, buddy. Keeps the hurt away. Don't you miss your wife?

ARTHUR: Of course.

WALLY: I wish she was here. She was nice.

ARTHUR: Yeah. I miss her, too.

MADGE storms in.

MADGE: WHAT THE HELL IS WRONG WITH YOU TWO?!

ARTHUR: Huh?

WALLY: Madge.

ARTHUR: *Makitohn* Madge. Hehe.

MADGE: WHAT THE HELL ARE YOU DOING? ARE YOU OUT OF YOUR DAMN MIND?!

ARTHUR: Calm yourself, holy.

MADGE: YOU! ARTHUR, THIS IS YOUR DOING! THOSE PEOPLE JUST LOST FAMILY IN A CAR ACCIDENT! THEY HAVE NOTHING AND YOU GO AND CHARGE THEM THREE HUNDRED DOLLARS.

WALLY: I'm sorry. I'm sorry…

ARTHUR: How do you know this?

MADGE: THEY TOLD ME!! SAID YOU DAMN NEAR BURNED THEM IN THE LODGE, INCLUDING TWO LITTLE GIRLS. DO YOU HAVE ANY SENSE?

ARTHUR: HEY!

MADGE: AND THEN YOU GO AND CHARGE THEM MONEY, YOU BASTARD!

ARTHUR: Go home.

MADGE: You're not getting away with this! You're not. Everyone's gonna know about this! Everyone.

ARTHUR: GET THE HELL OUT OF MY FRIEND'S HOUSE, WOMAN. OTHERWISE I'LL CALL THE RCs!

MADGE leans in.

MADGE: I dare you…

MADGE exits. Silence.

WALLY: Holy shit…

ARTHUR: Bitch.

WALLY: Holy shit, we're in trouble.

ARTHUR: No, no *nīciwakan*. We're good. We're good. Here, have a drink.

WALLY: There's no more.

ARTHUR: Really? Shit. Okay, well, let's go to the city.

WALLY: The city?

ARTHUR: Yeah, get out of here for a few days. 'Til Madge settles down. I'll phone my buddy, hire him to give us a ride. Hey?

WALLY: I don't know. I guess.

ARTHUR: Yeah. We'll get a hotel, some drinks, maybe some women. Be fun.

WALLY: Okay. Shit, buddy, I'm just drunk here. So we're good?

ARTHUR: Yeah, we're good. I'll, I'll talk with Madge in a few days. Fix it all up. Trust me.

WALLY: Okay. Hey, hey…Arthur…my son?

WALLY pulls a photo out of his pocket.

This my – my boy Darren. My boy.

ARTHUR: Heyyy. All right, Derek –

WALLY: No! DARREN, I said!

ARTHUR: Oh, okay. SORRY!

WALLY: Fuck THAT. FUCK YOU, I told you, DARREN.

ARTHUR: HEY! SETTLE DOWN! I JUST GOT YOU SOME WORK AND MONEY!

WALLY: Well, it's Darren…

ARTHUR: AND THIS IS HOW YOU TREAT ME? WHAT THE HELL? Looked like you were gonna hit me there for a second. Holy…

WALLY: …Sorry…Hey, buddy. Don't ditch me, okay? You gonna ditch me?

ARTHUR: What're you talking about?

WALLY: Don't ditch me.

ARTHUR: I'm not gonna ditch you. Come on, sing. We need more beers. Sing Bob Seger 'til a ride gets here.

WALLY: *Namoya.* I'll sing Hank. Or Johnny.

ARTHUR: This guy. Come on, sing something! It'll take a while for my buddy to get here. SING!

WALLY: Okay, I'll sing you my boy's favourite song.

Addresses the photo.

A song I wrote. For you, my boy.

Kisses the picture.

ARTHUR: Heyyy. All right. After that play some Bob Seger. Then we'll go to the city.

Flashback to the present.

Bugger even went and roughed up a woman cop later that night. Bet he didn't tell you that one, eh?

DARREN exits. WALLY attempts to leave.

Wally.

WALLY stops.

We're not done talking yet…

Scene 4

DARREN walks into the house and slams the door. He is trying to keep composed.

DARREN: Assholes! Both of them. Sons of bitches. He's dead. They're both dead. I don't care if I go back…I don't care…dead! Assholes…

He grabs the third beer from the fridge.

Who cares?

A knock on the door.

UGH! WHAT?! WHO IS IT?

CINDY is in the doorway.

Cindy?

CINDY: Hey.

DARREN: Fuck my life.

She enters.

Really, Cindy? Now!? What are you doing here?

CINDY: Long time no see. Nice to see you, too. I figured you'd be here.

DARREN: I told you not to come here!!

CINDY: Yeah, right before you hung up on me. Jerk! You think I'm here to get you back? Gimme some credit.

No reply from DARREN.

I'm passing through. Going up north…

DARREN: Well if you have anything to say, make it quick, 'cuz I'm going back to the pen.

CINDY: What?! What are you talking about?

DARREN: Make it quick, I said.

CINDY: This looks familiar.

DARREN paces.

What, someone look at you the wrong way? You getting ready to head out and mess someone up? Goddammit, Darren.

DARREN: You wouldn't understand. You never did.

CINDY: All right, well. Good luck and happy life. Too bad. You could've gotten to see your son one last time.

DARREN: I don't have time for this shit right now.

CINDY: Oh, this shit? Gawd…

You've got a lot of nerve. You know? I'm glad I ran into you. God, you're so damn arrogant –

DARREN: Yeah, shit. Always shit. Whenever I'm trying you gotta come around and fuck me up. Now this –

CINDY: I don't wanna do this! I don't. Gawd, DARREN!

Pause.

Look. Please. Believe it or not, it's good that I'm here.

DARREN: WHAT?!

Pause.

CINDY: I'm pregnant.

DARREN: I'm sure as hell glad it's not mine.

CINDY: Me too!

DARREN: That explains the mood swings. So, okay, uh, what?

CINDY: It's my fiance's. That's where I'm going. To see him.

DARREN: You're engaged?

CINDY: Yeah. See?

She shows him her ring.

DARREN: Couldn't wait for me, so now you're just making an instant family for my son.

CINDY: Oh, get real, please. I did wait. I waited! Two years.

DARREN: No, you didn't.

CINDY: Wake up! Are you really in that much denial? Darren, I wrote you. You never wrote back. No calls. Nothing. I waited. And waited. Then –

DARREN: So you came here to rub it in my face.

CINDY: That's not why.

DARREN: I'm looking for work!

CINDY: No. Not money.

DARREN: Well, you got me confused.

CINDY: Why didn't you call? Huh? Why? Were you afraid? Ashamed? Is that it?

No reply from DARREN.

That's it, isn't it? Ashamed. Okay. All right. Now I know.

Pause.

Darren. Look at you.

DARREN: Huh?

CINDY: Huh?! *(She gives him a soft punch in the gut.)* Gawd, you never listen.

DARREN: Michel?

CINDY: Come six months, Jake and I are going to be busy…

DARREN: Jake, pfft.

CINDY: Hey! We'll be preparing for the baby and the wedding. I need someone to take Michel for a while. I just wanted to see if that someone might be you. So, can you man up and be a dad?

Pause.

Can you, or what?

DARREN: Me? Really? Why?

CINDY: He's your son. And this way I can tell him I at least tried to keep his dad in his life. But just know: you screw up and you'll never see him again.

Well, that's a little extreme. But you won't see him for a while.

She shows DARREN her phone pics.

He's such a sweetheart. Top in his class. Girls just like him, too, and his long hair.

DARREN: Wow…So, really? What about my parole?

CINDY: I can keep quiet…

Pause.

My dad died…

DARREN: What?!

CINDY: My biological dad. I met him.

No reply from DARREN.

And just when I had taken Michel and made the move up north…he dies.

DARREN: Oh, my god…

CINDY: Yeah…

DARREN: Geez, Cindy, I –

CINDY: It's okay. Thanks. He was sick. My son – our son, lost his grandpa just over a year ago. I never told anyone.

DARREN: Shit. All right, what are the terms?

CINDY: I don't know, maybe I can drop him off the occasional weekend. So you two can get used to each other again. He keeps asking about you, his dad. Every boy needs his dad, Darren…every boy…

Pause.

Hey! Pregnant Métis woman here! Can you get your shit together, or what?!

DARREN: Uh, yeah. Yeah, I can do that, yeah…

CINDY: Good.

DARREN: I'm sorry about your dad.

CINDY: Look at you. You shouldn't be alone. You wanna come with me to see him?

DARREN: HE'S HERE? MICHEL?!

CINDY: Yeah. At Madge's. That's who told me you were here. I didn't wanna tell you right away. I know how mad you can get.

DARREN: I'm getting better at it…

CINDY: I'm going to pick him up. You can see him for a bit before we leave.

DARREN: Really?

CINDY: Come on, jerk…

DARREN: Okay…

They leave.

Scene 5

WALLY and ARTHUR are still sitting in the cafe.

ARTHUR: You? You're applying for an elder position? You?

WALLY: Yeah.

ARTHUR: That's funny.

WALLY: Why is that funny?

ARTHUR: You wouldn't know what to do.

WALLY: Same with you.

ARTHUR: No. I do know what I'm doing. That's the difference between us. I may not be one of these hardcore red-roaders, but I know how, and how to sell it. Just have people feel good, even if just for a little while. That's what's important.

WALLY: Unbelievable.

Pause.

ARTHUR: Oh, I ran into that cop.

WALLY: What cop?

ARTHUR: That woman cop. Remember? In the city? When we got drunk –

WALLY: I remember you ditching.

ARTHUR: I went back. To apologize. They gave me a slap on the wrist and let me go. Kept asking about you, though.

WALLY: And what did you tell them?

ARTHUR: Can't remember…

Pause.

Hmmm, you know, maybe you should apply for that elder job, Wally.

WALLY: What?

ARTHUR: Yeah. I know I have a better chance…

WALLY: You think?

ARTHUR: …but I really just need to keep low these days, you know.

WALLY: Yeah…

ARTHUR: A job like that could put me in the spotlight, anyway. I don't want any attention.

WALLY: Of course.

ARTHUR: And of course, you'll need help. I could come work for you. Pay me right and we could run some things together.

WALLY: My son really wanted to – Should've let him…

ARTHUR: Darwin.

WALLY: Geez. You just don't get it. I gotta go.

ARTHUR: No! You just don't get it! There is no authentic culture. Not anymore. The schools, priests, nuns and the church took it all away. They won.

WALLY: Good luck, Broken Wind.

WALLY turns to leave, then suddenly turns back.

Oh, and this is for my boy.

WALLY hits ARTHUR, who collapses to the floor.

His name's Darren. And thanks! Got it all.

WALLY shows ARTHUR his phone – which he has been recording on – turns it off, then leaves.

Scene 6

School hallway. MADGE finishes a prayer.

MADGE: *Mamawi-nohtawimaw kinanaskomitin* (My Creator, I thank you). *Hei hei.*

Tanisi kahkiyaw. Madge tipiskaw nitsiyihkason. Ekwa niya ohci asini ospwakan askihk. (Hello, everyone. My name is Madge Night and I'm from Stone Pipe First Nation.) My Cree name is *Mikisiw Pikiskwew Iskwew.* (Eagle Speaks Woman.) This name was given to me by my father, a sun dance maker, pipe carrier, and sweat lodge leader. I myself carry a master's degree in social work and a bachelor's degree in education.

I'm also very fortunate to have learned over three decades the teachings of my father's lodge and medicine council. It's with great honour that I accept the position as Stone Pipe School Elder. There is a lot of work that needs to be done here. Initially my plan was to move to the city, but there's been too much hardship here over the past few years. Tragedy, death, loss, hopelessness. I believe very much in our traditions to help us. I'm serious about our culture, language, and history. I'll be consulting with many cultural leaders about our ceremonies, practices, and protocol. To share not only with our youth, but with our community. So that we can move forward – step by step – in a good way, with good minds and good hearts. So with that, I thank you, and look forward to a new path for us all. *Kinanaskomitinawaw.* (Thank you all.) *Hei hei.*

Drum group sings a round dance song. DARREN and WALLY leave the gymnasium.

WALLY: *Miyo-kisikaw anohc.* (For sure. It's a good day.) Thanks for coming, son.

DARREN: I almost didn't. I really wanted to kick your ass. Good thing you let me be for a few days. I needed the time.

WALLY: Yeah. Was out at Madge's. Catching up. You know, I really like her words. About bringing back culture and language for the youth.

DARREN: I think she'll do good things.

WALLY: Step by step.

DARREN: I like that. Hey, no offence, but I'm glad Madge got the job and not you.

WALLY: *Nīsta mīna.* (Me too).

DARREN: Like, really glad.

WALLY: Uh huh. *Tapwe.*

DARREN: Really, really glad –

WALLY: Okay, son. That's good.

DARREN: So where's Broken Wind?

WALLY: Arthur. Bah, he probably took off. He's running out of places to hide. Think that's why he came back, except no one wants him back. He can't run and hide forever. Things catch up.

DARREN: How do you get all your information?

WALLY: Madge, who else?

DARREN: I'm really glad HE'S not in as elder, either.

WALLY: No damn kidding, eh?

DARREN: Geez, that would be horrible.

WALLY: I think someone punching him out changed his mind about staying.

DARREN: What? No way. Really? You?

WALLY: He deserved it…from Broken Wind to Broken Nose.

DARREN: Should've let me do it.

WALLY: And let you have all the fun? Plus I told him I got all our talk recorded…

DARREN: Really? You recorded all of it?

WALLY: No. Actually I don't know how to work it, but Arthur doesn't know that. *Asay ci? Ahaw, ekwa maka.* (Ready? Let's go.)

DARREN: Where?

WALLY: Home. There's a hockey game on. Figure I'll start watching.

DARREN: You're shitting me, right?

WALLY: Yes, yes, I am. Lodge is done, pit is dug. We gotta go get the wood and rocks.

DARREN: I knew there was something.

WALLY: Darren, how come you don't speak Cree?

DARREN: Mom always spoke it. I kinda quit after she passed on. Why do YOU speak it?

WALLY: The first sentence my own mom taught me was, *"Pako ta-ahakamik pīkiskweyak ōma ka-nehiyawewin."* (We need to continue speaking our Cree language.) When I heard how cool that sounded, I wanted to learn. So she taught me. It's important to know the language of our mothers.

DARREN: Maybe…

WALLY: If I can speak it, so can you. I'll teach you.

DARREN: Maybe, I said. Hey, Wally.

WALLY: *Kīkway*?

DARREN: Sorry I ditched on making that sweat lodge.

WALLY: It's okay. I should have come and visited you. I should have. I was just…ashamed. Like somehow it was my fault. You know, all these years, I felt like a big nothing.

DARREN: Really?

WALLY: When I first met your mom I told her, "*Iskwew,* I'm gonna make you mine. And I'm gonna build us a big lodge to live in." Ah, get lost, Tonto, she said. You have enough trouble trynna build character. In the end, I won her hand, but that crappy old Indian Affairs piece of shit house of ours is all I could get. And now it's starting to fall apart.

Pause.

I failed as a husband. You in jail? I failed as a father. I was alone. One night Arthur showed up, we did a sweat. Scored some cash, got some beers. I had one. Then another, and another. Only takes one, right? Then we went to the city. That woman cop. Pushed her. Grabbed her gun. I got scared. Used my compensation money to get a passport and jumped on a plane. Chiapas, Mexico. 'Cuz Mexico's where they go in the movies, eh? Met up with some gathering group of Indians, and it changed things for me. So I came back. Came back for you, and my grandson. That's what happened. That's the real story.

DARREN: Man, you know…years ago I would've just beat the shit out of you after that story. Honestly…

But I wanna be a father. A good one. To my son. One day he's gonna look at our world, the way we live now, and see the nonsense in it all. I just wanna make sure he has a decent life. While I still have a chance.

WALLY: *Metoni miywasin, nikosis.* (That is very good, son).

Darren? Son…I didn't know.

About the sweat.

About Arthur and what happened…

I didn't know…

I would have helped you or something…

My boy…

I'm so, so sorry…

Beat.

DARREN: Okay.

…I'm pissed off, but I'll get over it. I will. In time, I'll say *"metoni kayas."*

WALLY almost steps in for a hug.

But not now.

WALLY: Okay.

DARREN: Oh, hey.

WALLY: Yeah?

DARREN: That song? About take a chance. Dance, dance or something? The music was actually pretty good.

WALLY: I know, eh?

DARREN: But the lyrics suck.

WALLY: Oh…yeah…

DARREN: I mean, gawd, they're just horrible.

WALLY: Okay, son…

DARREN: …maybe we can work on that.

WALLY: Yeah?

DARREN: I gotta get to the rec centre. Round dance tonight. Floors are dirty.

WALLY: *Kayp.*

DARREN: See ya later…

Dad.

WALLY smiles. They take separate exits.

THE END

Glossary

Cree Word or Phrase	**English Approximation**
Ahaw/Aha	An expression of affirmation
Api ōta	Sit here
Asay ci	Are you ready?
Astam	Come
Ceskwa	Wait
Eee wah hua	An expression of surprise
Ekosi	That's it for now
Ekwa e-waskweyawin	He is part of his destiny
Ekwa maka	Let's go
Hei hei	Informal for "Thank you"
Holeh	Mispronunciation of "holy"
Iskwew	Woman
Kahkiyaw niwakomakanak	All my relations (prayer)
Kayas	Long ago
Kayp	Mispronunciation of "okay"
Kihkway	What
Kinanaskomitinawaw	Thank you all
Kinanaskōmitinawāw napewak ekwa iskwewak	Thank you, ladies and gentlemen
Kiya maka	And yourself?
Kohkom	Grandmother
Madge Tipiskaw nitsiyihkason	My name is Madge Night

Mahalo (Hawaiian)	Thank you
Mahti maka	That's enough
Makitohn	Big Mouth
Mamawi-nohtawimaw kinanaskomitin	My Creator, I thank you
Metoni	Exactly
Metoni kayas	A very long time ago
Mikisiw Pikiskwew Iskwew	Eagle Speaks Woman
Miyo-kisikaw anohc	Good day or good morning
Miywasin	It's good
Moniyaw	White man
Moniyaw iskwew	White woman
Mosōm	Grandfather
Moya nanitaw	Not bad
Mwestas	Later
Namoya	No
Nanaskimonawaw	Thanks
Napew	Man
Nech	An expression of surprise
Nehiyaw	Cree
Nehiyawewin	Cree language
Nicimos	My sweetheart
Niciwakan	My friend
Nikosis	My son
Nīsta mīna	Me too
Nitsiyihkason	My name
Niya ohci asini ospwakan askihk	I'm from Stone Pipe First Nation
Nīya ohci asini-ospwakanihk ōta	I'm from Stone Pipe
Nosimak	My grandchildren

Oskapew	Helper
Oweya	An expression of surprise
Pako ta-ahakamik pīkiskweyak ōma ka-nehiyawewin	We need to continue speaking our Cree language
Peyakwan	Same
Picikwās, Picikwāsak	Apple, Apples
Pihtikwe	Come inside
Pimihāwi-pīsim	Autumn moon
Sēmak	Hurry
Soniyaw	Money
Taguy	Penis
Tanisi kahkiyaw	How are you all?
Tānisi kahkiyaw kīyawaw	Hello all, how are you?
Tanisi kīya	How are you?
Tapwe ci	It's true
Tawaw	Welcome
Wacistakac	An expression of surprise
Wacistakats	An expression of surprise
Waposomīcimapoy	Rabbit soup